How to use this book

Follow the advice, in italics, where given.

Support the children as they read the text that is shaded in cream.

Praise *the children at every step!*

Detailed guidance is provided in the Read Write Inc. Phonics Handbook.

Activity 8 (Answer the 'questions to read and answer') only appears in Sets 4–7.

---

8 reading activities

Children:

1 *Practise reading the speed sounds.*
2 *Read the green and red words for the non-fiction text.*
3 *Listen as you read the introduction.*
4 *Discuss the vocabulary check with you.*
5 *Read the non-fiction text.*
6 *Re-read the non-fiction text and discuss the 'questions to talk about'.*
7 *Re-read the non-fiction text with fluency and expression.*
9 *Practise reading the speed words.*

Speed sounds

Consonants *Say the pure sounds (do not add 'uh').*

f ff	l (ll)	m mm	n nn kn	r rr	s ss	v (ve)	z zz s	sh	th	ng nk

b bb	c k ck	d dd	g gg	h	j g ge	p pp	qu	t tt	w wh	x	y	(ch) (tch)

Vowels *Say the vowel sound and then the word, e.g. 'a', 'at'.*

at	hen head	in	on	up	day	see happy	high	blow

zoo	look	car	for	fair	whirl	shout	boy

*Each box contains one sound but sometimes more than one grapheme. Focus graphemes are **circled**.*

Green words

Read in Fred Talk (pure sounds).

h<u>igh</u>	n<u>igh</u>t	m<u>igh</u>t	s<u>igh</u>t	fl<u>igh</u>t	tr<u>ee</u>
f<u>ee</u>t	d<u>ee</u>p	s<u>ee</u>m	gr<u>ee</u>dy	grip	bran<u>ch</u>
ha<u>ve</u>					

Read in syllables.

a` w<u>ay</u>  →  aw<u>ay</u>        tim` id   → timid

an` i` mal → animal   fr<u>igh</u>t` en` <u>ing</u> → fr<u>igh</u>ten<u>ing</u>

Read the root word first and then with the ending.

sl<u>ee</u>p → sl<u>ee</u>ping   tel<u>l</u> → tel<u>l</u>ing   t<u>igh</u>t → t<u>igh</u>tly

pi<u>tch</u> → pi<u>tch</u>ed

Red words

the   call   to   of   makes*

winter*   ears*   echo*   good*

*red for this book only

Bats

Introduction

Have you ever seen a bat?
They are called nocturnal animals
because they sleep in the daytime
and come out at night. Can you
think of any other nocturnal
animals? Read this batty book
to find out all about bats!

Written by Gill Munton

Vocabulary check

Discuss the meaning (as used in the non-fiction text) after the children have read the word.

	definition
timid	*very shy*
high-pitched	*a very high sound, e.g. a shriek*
in flight	*when something is flying*
echo	*a sound that bounces off an object and comes back*

Punctuation to note:

Bats This	Capital letters that start sentences
.	Full stop at the end of each sentence
,	Comma to show a pause
!	Exclamation mark

A bat might seem frightening.

But a bat is a timid animal.

Sleeping

Bats sleep in the day.

This bat is sleeping high up in a tree. Its feet grip the branch tightly.

In winter, bats have a long, deep sleep, away from bright lights.

Night flights

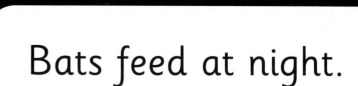

Bats feed at night.

A bat has good sight,
but at night it needs its ears!

call

It makes a high-pitched call when it is in flight.

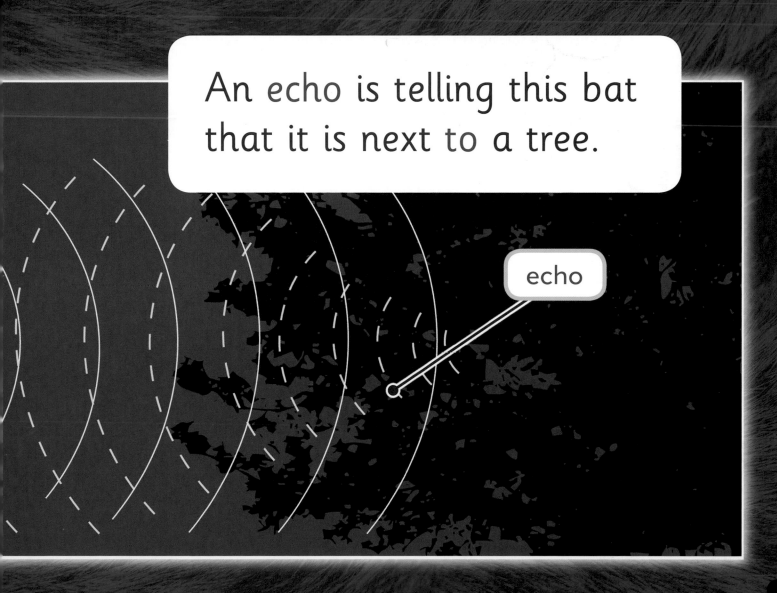

Feeding

This bat feeds on insects.

A greedy bat might snap up hundreds of insects in a night!

Questions to talk about

Re-read the page. Read the question to the children. Tell them whether it is a FIND IT *question or* PROVE IT *question.*

FIND IT	PROVE IT
✓ Turn to the page	✓ Turn to the page
✓ Read the question	✓ Read the question
✓ Find the answer	✓ Find your evidence
	✓ Explain why

Page 9:	PROVE IT	*Do you think a bat is likely to attack you?*
Pages 10–11:	FIND IT	*When do bats sleep?*
Page 12:	FIND IT	*When do bats eat?*
Page 13:	FIND IT	*What does a bat need at night?*
Page 14:	FIND IT	*What type of call does a bat make?*
Page 16:	FIND IT	*What do bats like to eat?*

Speed words

Children practise reading the words across the rows, down the columns and in and out of order clearly and quickly.

high	need	grip	have	timid
branch	away	night	feet	animal
deep	flight	tree	insect	that
up	greedy	might	next	from
bat	tight	the	snap	sight